THE ILLEGAL ALIEN FROM MEXICO

The Illegal Alien from Mexico

POLICY CHOICES FOR AN INTRACTABLE ISSUE

by Sidney Weintraub
and Stanley R. Ross

Mexico–United States Border Research Program
THE UNIVERSITY OF TEXAS AT AUSTIN

International Standard Book Number 0-292-73822-6
Library of Congress Catalog Card Number 80-80323
Copyright © 1980 by the Mexico–United States Border
    Research Program, The University of Texas at Austin
Printed in the United States of America

Distributed by the University of Texas Press,
Post Office Box 7819, Austin, Texas 78712

Contents

Preface   *vii*

I. Reasons for Another Look   *3*

II. The "Facts"   *8*

III. The Choices on the United States Side   *21*

IV. Treat the Cause and Not the Symptoms   *44*

V. Conclusions   *52*

References   *57*

Preface

DURING THE SUMMER OF 1976 a meeting was convened at Cuernavaca, Morelos, at the invitation of the Mexican National Council of Science and Technology (CONACYT) to discuss policy-oriented research on border problems affecting the relations between Mexico and the United States. Lic. Gerardo Bueno, then Director of CONACYT, led a delegation of Mexican officials, institutional representatives, and researchers, while the undersigned was privileged to lead the delegation from the United States.

In those discussions we achieved agreement on a program of broadly defined research priorities with the understanding that national priorities and available resources, both human and financial, would affect the focus on each side of the border and that projects might be individual, parallel, or joint as the circumstances warranted. There were pledges of cooperation and of dissemination of the results of the research.

It is in that spirit that the United States part of the binational Mexico–United States Border Research Program offers this, the first in a series of publications. This specific effort was undertaken for two reasons. The sponsoring foundation was interested in having the existing research literature on Mexican illegal migration reviewed and the current state of our knowledge assessed. Secondly, the essay is a response to an awareness that there is often a problem of synchronization between the informational needs of policymakers and the time necessary to achieve results from academic research. Policymakers have to develop and implement policy for this week, this month, and this year, while research may involve two or more years for data gathering and analysis before publication.

As a consequence, Professor Weintraub and I decided to undertake a review of the existing research literature on Mexican illegal migration and to examine the available policy alternatives in the light of the current state of our knowledge. In the process we believe that the shortcomings of existing data and the complications of Mexican–U.S. interaction have been highlighted.

These preliminary remarks would not be complete without acknowledging our indebtedness to those who made the study and its publication possible. First, we are indebted to Mr. Gilbert Denman and the Ewing Halsell Foundation for confidence in our efforts and for the grant under which this project was carried out. Second, we are appreciative for the support and encouragement of the authorities at the University of Texas at Austin who authorized participation in this binational effort and provided the program coordinator with support needed to implement this program.

Last, but by no means least, I wish to take this opportunity to dedicate this initial study of the Mexico–United States Border Research Program to the mem-

ory of the late Ambassador Vicente Sánchez Gavito
—distinguished Mexican diplomat and outstanding
human being—who served as the initial Mexican coordinator for this program and did so much to insure that
it would get under way.

Stanley R. Ross, *Coordinator*
Mexico–United States Border Research Program

THE ILLEGAL ALIEN FROM MEXICO

I. Reasons for Another Look

THE ISSUE of illegal or undocumented migration from Mexico has become a matter of public consciousness and concern. President Carter focused national attention on the problem, but his tackling of the issue was rewarded with almost universal criticism. The president's 1977 legislative package is now dead. In its place, Congress established a Select Committee on Immigration to examine total immigration policy and report back after two years.

Organized labor complained that the president's proposals did not go far enough to minimize the impact of millions of migrants on the labor market at a time of high unemployment for secondary or unskilled labor; land owners felt they needed Mexican workers to pick fruits, vegetables, and other crops at harvest time; many small businessmen, such as restaurant owners, feared they could not survive without the illegal workers; industrial employers argued that they did not wish to be policemen to verify the *bona fides* of prospective workers; many citizens objected to amnesty (or alteration of status) provisions on the grounds that they rewarded lawbreaking. At the same time Mexican-American organizations objected because the amnesty provisions were not generous enough and would place in limbo for five years a group who would be neither permanent resident aliens nor illegal migrants; in addition many Mexican-Americans were concerned that the employer punishment provisions would exacerbate discrimination against all Hispanics. Civil libertarians shared Mexican-American concern about increased ethnic discrimination and feared that an improved social security card or other identification document included in the proposal to take civil action against employers who repeatedly hired undocumented workers would be the opening wedge to a universal identity card system. U.S. zero population advocates saw millions of human beings being added to the United States' population, increasing pressure on jobs, resources, and the environment (*New York Times*, 1977*a*; Wierken, 1977). Many Americans who took pride in our open borders with our nearest neighbors were concerned that amnesty now must lead to a less open border in order to prevent the need for repetitive cycles of amnesty in the future; and those concerned with United States relations with Mexico were convinced that unilateral actions by the United States would only exacerbate the existing tensions in United States–Mexican relations.

It was this chorus of criticism as well as the growing pressure to come to grips with the problem that prompted this detailed examination of the literature and of options in dealing with illegal migration from Mexico. As one might expect, much of the carping leveled at the administration proposal was self-interested; this did not make it invalid, but certainly made it suspect. Even a cursory review of existing research reveals how easy it is for the analyst to become an advocate. We have no personal involvement in the issue and can at least try to be dispassionate in our analysis.

Our excuse for jumping in where others have been burned is that the issue is important and is likely to be increasingly so. The movement of Mexicans to the United States supplies the kind of escape valve that emigration always has provided—to the Irish coming to the United States at a time of famine, for instance, and to Jews at times of persecution. The emigration valve helps to relieve pressure on the home country and may even involve survival for emigrating individuals (as we have seen in Viet Nam). The remittances sent back to Mexico by emigrants have been a significant positive element (although the precise amount is unknown) in the current account of Mexico's balance of payments, not to speak of the importance to the receiving families, many of them in impoverished areas of Mexico. The illegal immigrants may not compete across the entire U.S. labor market, but they certainly must affect the secondary labor market. Texas, for example, is a right-to-work state and the per capita income in some of the poorest border counties is about 50 percent of that for the United States as a whole; surely these facts must in part be the consequence of employers' ability to obtain Mexicans who, as Ray Marshall put it, work "scared and hard" (Marshall, 1978*b*). Wholesale evasion of the law must inevitably breed contempt for the law. We ended Prohibition for this very reason.

There is another side (many other sides) to these arguments. The system of illegal migration from Mexico that now exists works to meet needs of many undocumented workers and their employers as well as those of the Mexican government and society. An article in the Mexico City newspaper *Excélsior* brought out the importance of this issue to Mexico; it noted that about one of four Mexicans in the work force is working in the United States (*Excélsior*, 1978). The figure seems high, but even one in five or six would be a remarkable number. Tampering with the current system could make a bad situation worse; and we have an extensive history of making bad things worse (as in Viet Nam). Why not leave bad enough alone?* The illegal migration problem has no complete solution. At best, the president's program would affect certain elements of the problem, but, judging from the criticism it has aroused, would do this at the cost of worsening other aspects. Most serious of all is the feeling that, in all likelihood, its measures would not have resulted in reduction of the migrant flow. This is true of many suggested solutions of this issue; the outcomes may be as intended or precisely the reverse.

We propose in this essay to subject the various policy options to analysis in the light of the known facts. Unfortunately many of the most important facts are not known. We often make national policy in ignorance (we did so in Viet Nam, and we have tampered repeatedly with our public education system with only the faintest notion of the consequences), but there must

*A cartoon in the *Wall Street Journal* of April 24, 1978, shows one man at a bar saying to another: "Remember the good old days when problems had solutions?"

be some threshold of knowledge before far-reaching programs affecting millions of people should be set into motion. We may not have crossed the knowledge threshold on this issue and we therefore believe that modesty is called for when proposing action.

We will make policy suggestions, but our major recommendation is to exercise caution in taking drastic action. We do not advocate inaction (although we think this would be preferable to certain action), but neither do we think that a moral crusade would be desirable. We also doubt the effectiveness of policy measures taken without Mexican cooperation, and the president's program, or any unilateral program, will not produce this essential element.

II. The "Facts"

BEFORE TRYING to solve a problem, it is useful to know its dimensions. Much of our knowledge is based on partial or skewed data and surveys which are extrapolated to a universe based on what at best can charitably be called heroic assumptions. It is not that we don't know anything, but that we don't know very much. Leonel Castillo, Commissioner of Immigration and Naturalization, admits that we do not know how many illegal migrants are in the country (*Austin American Statesman*, 1977), and the White House Domestic Council's task force which drafted the Carter proposal admitted that "a dramatic lack of information makes analysis of illegal migration impossible at this time" (U.S. Department of Justice, 1976).

It is generally known that much of our "hard" data on illegals entering the country are based on Immigration and Naturalization Service (INS) apprehensions. In U.S. fiscal year 1977 there were over a million apprehensions (INS, 1977d), representing a 20 percent increase over the preceding year and the first time that the million figure was exceeded since 1954. The rapid growth of apprehensions, a 500 percent increase over a decade earlier, is indicative of a rising number of undocumented aliens. However, such data tell us precious little about the number of real people actually crossing the border. How many of these are repeat apprehensions? The INS data collection system does not tell us this. Except for anecdotal narratives of individuals caught twice or three times within a short period, or other bits of individual evidence that after the first or second failure the INS ceases to be as formidable an adversary, the rest is guesswork. How many make it for each person caught? The best that we can do is to rely on "expert" judgment that asserts that for every apprehension, two or three or four get across the border scot free. Does this mean that one million, two million, four million, cross each year? The differences among these numbers are significant, and the honest answer is that we don't know.

Our analysis focuses on Mexican undocumented aliens, but they are by no means the only illegal migrants. The INS lists sixty nations as sources of illegals, with the Dominican Republic, Haiti, Jamaica, and Guatemala following Mexico as principal sources (INS, 1977c). The Caribbean migrants enter largely through Florida and New York, sometimes without examination, often with forged documents, or by overstaying temporary visas. Many South and Central Americans enter via Mexico. For these sending countries the number of migrants is as important demographically and economically as for Mexico. However, movement back and forth across the long border between Mexico and the United States involves more people, has a long history, and also tends to be easier. It should be kept in mind that any policy adopted will affect more than Mexico and Mexicans.

About 90 percent of the illegal migrants that the

INS catches are Mexicans (INS, 1977d). This high percentage is a consequence of the INS concentration of its border patrol and apprehension activities on the Mexican border and on areas where Mexicans congregate. Despite this concentration, the number of non-Mexican Latin Americans who are apprehended each year rises. Skin color does make a difference and adds to the emotionalism of this issue. To use the official nomenclature, most apprehended illegals are EWIs, those who enter without inspection (these accounted for more than 90 percent of the total for U.S. fiscal year 1977), since that is how most Mexican illegals enter (INS, 1977d). There is substantial evidence that many illegals, particularly from other countries, come here on valid visas and then overstay their permitted time and are not apprehended. How many of these people are there? The United States government believes that about 60 percent of the illegals who remain in the United States are Mexicans (U.S. Department of Justice, 1978). We really do not know this to be accurate because of the lack of controls on nonimmigrants after entry into the United States.

We don't know, therefore, how many illegal immigrants enter the United States each year, either as EWIs or otherwise, or how many are Mexicans. The total number entering is substantial—that much we know from apprehension records—but just how substantial remains a matter of guesswork.

This is only part of our ignorance. Those illegals who come, find jobs, and then go home, perhaps to repeat this process many times, obviously render a service (perhaps at the expense of the lowest income groups in our society, a point to which we will return) and probably stimulate economic growth in our country. The post–World War II growth in many European countries, such as Switzerland and West Germany, could not have been as great without temporary (not illegal) workers who were contracted for in good times and then were dismissed in bad times, although many of them have stayed on rather than return to their country of origin. We, of course, have done the same; we have encouraged workers to come here in times of labor shortage, such as during World War II, and then forced most of them home when times were less prosperous, as in the depression years of 1930–33 and in "Operation Wetback" in 1953–54. It is not accidental, we believe, that the current hullabaloo about illegal migrants started at a time of high unemployment in the United States. Most Americans take advantage of the services that illegals render; for example, our fruits and vegetables are undoubtedly cheaper than they would be if the illegals were not available for this work. Whether we should want cheaper food under these circumstances is a separate issue, but we accept the implicit subsidy nonetheless.

Those who come and eventually do not go home, whatever their original intent, pose a different kind of problem. They become part of the regular work force rather than serve the buffer function (a phrase borrowed from Professor Marios Nikolinakos of the Free University of Berlin) of coming when needed and being dismissed when not wanted. Whatever one may argue about labor force competition between legal United States residents and temporary workers who come and go breaks down when one discusses permanent entrants into the labor force, whether they are here illegally or not. The number of illegals who have been here long enough to be considered permanent is unknown, and the estimates are so disparate as to be useless. In presenting the president's program, the administration asserted that there are between three and five million illegal immigrants of all nationalities residing in the United States, and that this number is increasing by about half a million persons a year. The administration further asserted that about one-third of the Mexicans who enter illegally take up permanent residence, whereas the majority of those illegals coming from other countries generally do so with the intention of remaining permanently (U.S. Department of Justice, 1978). However, estimates made by official and unofficial researchers of the number of illegals permanently living here are much larger, ranging between two and about twelve million. The number of Mexicans has been estimated variously from five or six million downwards. In its amnesty, or adjustment of status proposal, the administration proposed two categories. In one, permanent resident status was granted to illegals here prior to January 1, 1970, and in the other, a five-year temporary resident status was established for those here before January 1, 1977. The former would represent the fourth updating of the register since the country began to control and restrict immigration in 1924. The last such updating took place in 1965 and made aliens resident in the country since 1948 eligible for adjustment of status. While the earlier adjustments affected thousands and it took three such adjustments to move up the date two decades, the Carter proposal would advance the date twenty-two years (1948 to 1970) and is estimated to affect millions. The intention of the second provision was to encourage the illegals who came during the seven-year period (1970–77) to register so that we could count them. Attorney General Bell, in suggesting this purpose, added that once the number was known a decision could be made on a more permanent solution (Marshall, Bell, Castillo, 1977). Most observers consider it unlikely that undocumented workers would come forth under this arrangement. What evidence we do have based on apprehensions suggests that the mere news of the proposed program brought an upsurge of entries and a flourishing business in forged documents to prove earlier residence.

One of the most frequently cited studies about the habits of Mexican illegals is that of Wayne Cornelius of the Massachusetts Institute of Technology (Cornelius, 1976). He and a colleague conducted extended interviews of 80 residents, made a population census of 2,960 households, and searched local records in the region of Los Altos in the state of Jalisco. This particular agricultural region was chosen because of its long history of emigration, both to other locations in Mexico and to the United States. From this sample Cornelius found that migration from these communities to the United States generally was of a temporary character and that the average length of stay in the United States was about six to eight months, usually from March to early December. There are other instances of migrants remaining up to two and three years and a few even longer. The December date for returns suggests holiday visits to family in a slack agricultural period in the United States.

About 60 percent of migrants in Cornelius' sample worked in the United States as agricultural labor and seemed to progress into nonagricultural work as they gained experience through successive illegal entries. His description of the people in his sample at a particular time is valid. But is it valid to extrapolate from this limited group at given times who returned home, to all Mexican illegals, from all destinations, at all times, to justify an assertion that most illegals prefer to maintain a pattern of seasonal migration? This assertion, or some variant of it, is common, particularly by those who opposed the president's program (Cornelius, 1978a). Research at El Colegio de México, which is by no means definitive, indicates that migration from different regions in Mexico exhibits different characteristics (Alba, 1978). Those coming from more urban areas in Mexico tend not to return home. A San Antonio researcher, Ron Grennes, has found that migrants from urban centers like Mexico City and Puebla tend to remain longer, even permanently (Grennes, 1977). In any event, we are dealing with a dynamic phenomenon, with apparently more and more people coming across the Mexican border illegally every year, from more and more original locations, so that a typical pattern of 1976 may not be valid for 1977 after the Mexican peso was devalued, and may not be valid for 1978 when new habits were superimposed on already changing past habits and new kinship patterns were established in the United States.

14

Another disturbing feature about the surveys on which much evidence available to us is based is that most of them were conducted among apprehended illegal migrants. The samples admittedly are not random. Are those illegal migrants who are apprehended typical of those who are not caught, or is this like describing the habits of wild animals from observing their behavior in captivity? The Julian Samora (Samora, 1971) study on the wetbacks, the David North and Marion Houstoun study on illegal aliens in the labor market (North and Houstoun, 1976), the Vic Villalpando et al. study with its attempt to obtain a profile of the illegal aliens in San Diego County (Villalpando et al., 1977), all drew their sample (in the case of North and Houstoun, most of their sample) from detention centers. (The Mexican Labor Ministry has been conducting surveys among Mexicans who were deported or were permitted to return home voluntarily. This, too, is a biased sample.) It is unfair to criticize this practice, since there is no ready alternative; unapprehended illegals still in the United States do not like to talk to academic or government researchers about their habits. Unfortunately, however, as the researchers themselves mostly recognize, this does make suspect the generalizations that are derived. Villalpando's sample of 217 was all male. One of his findings was that 53 percent of those interviewed said they preferred to live in their native country and 39 percent said they preferred to live in the United States. Is this valid for all illegals? Is it even valid for those who answered the question in a detention center since the answer almost certainly contained a calculation of what it was thought the interviewer wanted to hear.

The apprehended Mexican illegal is mostly adult male (83 percent in U.S. fiscal year 1977 [INS, 1977*b*]) and the conventional wisdom is therefore that the Mexican illegal is predominantly male. North and Houstoun have pointed out that this conclusion is suspect since most of the INS enforcement staff is male and its members tend to focus on where males congregate (such as construction sites). In addition, apprehending a female illegal can be a nuisance since there are no overnight detention centers for them and they have to be lodged in jails at INS expense. There also is evidence that male enforcement officers are apprehensive about charges of sexual molestation by female detainees. The reason for the all male sample in the Villalpando study was precisely the lack of a detention facility for females at the Chula Vista border station; the females and children were placed on buses and escorted directly across the border to Tijuana.

Relevant hard facts are so scarce that even soft "facts" are seized upon and repeated endlessly until repetition makes them commonplace and therefore acceptable. Whatever appears in print is often taken as proven and true. One well-known example of this was the figure of 8.2 million illegals in this country, of whom 5.2 million were Mexican, contained in a report prepared by Lesko Associates for the INS and a summary of which was released in late 1975 (Lesko, 1975). This number found its way into the major American news media and into the mouths of government officials. The study no longer is given much credence because of doubtful statistical techniques (Roberts et al., 1978; Bustamante, 1976*c*), and it plays no role in current United States government calculations, but its earlier dissemination is typical of what occurs in this field.

Cornelius tried to estimate the level of remittances from the illegal immigrants to their families by taking a single day's remittance data of a large bank with many offices (Cornelius, 1976). On a recent trip to Mexico, we heard this figure, which is useful for its purposes, extrapolated for a full year and multiplied by all Mexican banks based on that one bank's percentage of banking transactions in Mexico, being cited as the figure for annual remittances by illegals. The estimate may be close, or it may be radically inaccurate, as Mexican investigators at the Ministry of Labor believe (Zazueta, 1978). The inherent error potential in this technique is immense. Official Bank of Mexico data on net unrequited transfers show about $188 million in 1977; North and Houstoun in their March 1976 study felt that a figure of $1.5 billion for annual remittances by illegals was then a reasonable estimate; extending Cornelius' figure as indicated comes to a total close to the North and Houstoun estimate, and this is given as verification of the magnitude of remittances. Indeed, comparability of data of two limited studies was taken as validation both by the analysts and others. The newspaper *Excélsior*, in describing a meeting on undocumented migration in Guadalajara, reported that remittances amounted to almost $3 billion annually, assuming greater importance than tourism (*Excélsior*, 1978). The official figure for net tourism income for 1977 was $470 million.

Finally, the most uncertain question is that of impact on the labor market. Among the conclusions in the North and Houstoun study, appropriately stated in the conditional form, is that the illegals appear to increase the supply of low-wage labor and compete with disadvantaged U.S. workers, and that the major immediate impact of illegals in the United States today is probably on the labor market. Vernon Briggs, who has studied the impact of illegals on the labor market in Texas, is convinced that the presence of a sizeable number of illegal aliens helps to explain the high unemployment rate in South Texas, the presence of the three poorest SMSAs (standard metropolitan statistical areas) in the United States, the poorest counties in Texas, the fact that the minimum wage is the prevailing wage in many occupations, the high use of food stamps and welfare assistance, and scant union activity (Briggs, 1976). These are all indirect forms of evidence, but based on much research. Barton Smith and Robert Newman of the University of Houston tried econometrically to compare wages in three Texas border SMSAs with those in Houston (Smith and Newman, 1977). Their data show that "resident Mexican-Americans and low-skill workers . . . are impacted much more than other workers," but that real income differentials between the border SMSAs and Houston are less than one might have expected after the cost of living is factored into the calculation.

However, it is the opposite assertion that is most troublesome because of the scanty research on which it is based. Cornelius has declared that there is no direct evidence (or smoking gun, so to speak) that large numbers of American workers have been displaced by illegal immigrants—certainly not from desirable jobs (Cornelius, 1978a). The evidence for this view comes primarily from two citations in the Villalpando study.

The first was a program conducted in Los Angeles, in which the authorities reportedly tried to place local residents in the jobs formerly held by apprehended illegals, and failed because the jobs paid less than the minimum wage and the job categories were unappealing. The second was an effort to place local residents of San Diego in jobs held by illegals; the jobs were filled instead by commuters (i.e., *legal* border crossers) from Tijuana, Mexico. It is a peculiar kind of rationalization that argues that no serious damage is done because only nondesirable jobs are lost and that legal U.S. residents cannot really have been hurt since they refused to accept less than the minimum wage in particular jobs at particular locations. Further, such reasoning gives little or no consideration to the numbers of aliens legalizing their situation by various means and showing upward mobility as they climb the economic ladder to more desirable positions.

What would happen if the supply of illegal immigrants were cut off and the minimum wage laws were rigorously enforced? We do not advocate this, but we ask what we think is a relevant question. Economic analysis would lead one to conclude that two forces would come into play: one force, by reducing the supply, should increase the price of labor; the second, by increasing the price of labor, might lead to more efficient management of production and greater use of labor-saving machinery. The second consequence cannot be analyzed effectively on a macro basis but instead would require some knowledge of machinery efficiency and costs (initial investment, maintenance, depreciation, replacement) and how efficiently production is organized as opposed to increased labor costs in different forms of activity in which illegal immigrants formerly were used.

As a nation, we do not know the labor market impact, and this really is the crux of the issue. The illegal immigration from Mexico, for a variety of reasons to which we will come, hits hardest on the secondary labor market, on those poor people least able to cope or to compete. How much it is hurting them is in dispute, but that it does affect them is clear. Of all our areas of ignorance, this is the most poignant in terms of human impact. The reactions of the people most seriously affected by the influx of illegals—the Mexican-Americans—are emotionally complex. As Americans of Mexican origin, they have kinship ties with the illegals and want them to come. They may wish to build the Hispanic population in the United States. As an underclass of impoverished Americans, they know that the supply of labor for many of the jobs they are able to fill is excessive in part because of the inflow of illegals. This conflicted response was typified by the reaction of César Chávez, head of the farmworkers union, who initially took a position in favor of restricting illegal immigration because of unionization and economic reasons, and then shifted position after pressure from the leaders of Mexican-American institutions. We know how these leaders feel; they are opposed for political as well as emotional reasons to measures that would effectively restrict the flow of Mexicans, illegal or otherwise, to the United States, although they do not phrase their position that way. We do not know the views of those most likely to be affected by the flow of illegals.

III. The Choices on the United States Side

IT IS HARD for a government to do nothing when its laws are openly flouted. There is no uniformity of opinion as to what action should be taken, but then there rarely is in as complex a human, economic, and social problem as this. Although the Congress has been addressing the illegal migration question for half a dozen years, legislative initiatives have suffered crippling amendments and none has been enacted. The record at the state level is hardly better.

The INS over the years has sought more funds to uphold the law, to prevent illegal immigration and to deport (or to permit voluntary departure of) those who break the law. The INS is not a well-funded agency. North has noted that the metropolitan police in the District of Columbia had 4,341 persons in October 1976 compared with 2,937 enforcement personnel for the INS; in fiscal year 1977, he noted that Congress authorized the employment of 1,140 policemen to guard the buildings on Capitol Hill (North, 1977). Former Attorney General John Mitchell, in talking about the Nixon administration, once said that people should watch what the administration did rather than what its officials said. This is apt for assessing the role we want for the INS.

21

Nor is the law, or justice, blind in its treatment of all the parties. It is against the law for a Mexican seeking economic improvement to cross into the United States without documentation. It is not against the law for an employer to hire an illegal alien. Harboring an illegal immigrant is illegal, but under the so-called Texas Proviso to the Immigration and Nationality Act, giving him employment is deemed not to be harboring. One can rationalize these provisions, since employers are not intended to be law enforcers, but they also turn out to be economically convenient for some powerful groups in our society. One can assume that the Texas interests who devised the Texas Proviso, and the comparable interests in other states such as California, are not deeply interested in seeing the INS built up enough to enforce the law effectively. Elwyn Stoddard of the University of Texas at El Paso has discussed this point (Stoddard, 1976).

The labor unions generally would like restrictions on the inflow of illegal immigrants, but as already noted, this is not now the formal position of the largely Chicano farmworkers' union. Many church groups argue in favor of open borders because this permits a natural international process of self-improvement of Mexicans. From time to time the Mexican government has argued in favor of a new *bracero* program (formally contracting Mexicans, up to a stated ceiling, to work at particular places) since this gives the governmental authorities some inspection rights and some control over treatment of Mexican nationals; and, unfortunately, it also gives greater opportunity for *mordidas* or graft.

The Echeverría administration in 1974 publicly deplored maltreatment of undocumented workers and suggested a return to a contract labor arrangement. When the Ford administration rejected this approach, the Mexican president dropped the matter (*New York Times*, 1974*a*, *b*; Echeverría, 1976). The Mexican ambassador to the United States repeated this suggestion early in 1979. However, the Carter administration has repeatedly stated its opposition to any such arrangement. When, in the spring of 1977, the president overruled the Department of Labor and ordered the admission of some 800 Mexican nationals for six months to harvest melons and vegetables near Presidio, Texas, as an emergency measure, it was specifically stated that the action was not the harbinger of a new *bracero* program (*New York Times*, 1977*b*; *Dallas Times Herald*, 1977).

The Carter administration did try to pick its way through the welter of competing opinions and interests, and this explains many of the compromises (e.g., civil rather than criminal penalties for employers) as well as the complexities in the proposed legislation (e.g., the limbo provision for illegals without going to an explicit identification or work permit system). The issues are complex, and we propose to sift through the major options.

1. *Don't Just Do Something, Sit There*

This is an appealing option: when ignorant, listen and learn since taking action only demonstrates the ignorance to all. There are also substantive arguments in favor of this position. *The Wall Street Journal*, in an editorial on June 18, 1976, summarized the most significant of these by noting that the supply of illegals "may well be providing the margin of survival for entire sectors of the economy" like restaurants, other small businesses, and both small- and large-scale agriculture, that rely heavily on unskilled labor. Harold Wool, in a report for the Department of Labor, projected the U.S. labor supply to 1985 and concluded that there will be potential shortages for lower-level occupations (Wool, 1976), so that future needs for immigrants (or for labor-saving techniques) may be greater than now exist. The major argument for doing nothing, therefore, rests on the calculus that the benefits from this supply of people in the secondary labor market outweigh the costs to domestic labor and the burdens on our social services and on our social fabric by retaining laws that we know will not be enforced, or will be enforced discriminatorily (i.e., mainly against dark-skinned persons, and mainly in times of domestic economic slowdown).

With regard to the direct burden on our social services, this is one of the few areas where the evidence is clear; most illegal workers have taxes deducted from their earnings (in the San Diego study, the interviews indicated that illegals contributed 17 percent of their wages to taxes) while their demands on social services (police costs, hospitals, food stamps, welfare, burial services, education in the public schools) are not great. The San Diego study is a significant one since, as the report notes, "San Diego is the most impacted area in the world by the flow of illegal aliens." San Diego accounts for 43 percent of all border apprehensions of illegal immigrants and 25 percent of apprehensions throughout the nation. The Villalpando study concluded that the cost to provide social services for illegals was $2 million a year, whereas tax contributions amounted to almost $49 million. The exact percentages are less significant than the orders of magnitude.

The Villalpando evidence is supported by the North and Houstoun inquiry. Based on their interviews with apprehended illegals, 77 percent had social security taxes withheld, 73 percent Federal income taxes, 44 percent hospitalization, and 31 percent even filed income tax returns. This is contrasted with 27 percent using hospitals, 4 percent who collected one or more weeks of unemployment insurance, 4 percent who had children in U.S. schools, 1 percent who secured food stamps, and less than 1 percent who received welfare payments. The requests of school authorities in south Texas for aid for their "impacted" districts suggest that the educational impact may be underestimated in some areas. Again, the exact percentages are less significant (since there would seem to be a natural tendency for the illegals to overstate their payments and understate their use of public services) than the orders of magnitude. The proposed amnesty provision would make those affected eligible for such services and would eliminate the reluctance to exercise their rights.

These findings are consistent with the Marshall "work scared and hard" aphorism; one would expect illegal immigrants to be compliant and not demanding. Persons who wish to restrict the inflow of illegals have argued that while the direct costs of social services to illegals may not be high in comparison to what they contribute, there may be nonmeasurable indirect costs. If illegal immigrants displace national labor and the latter must resort to welfare, food stamps, and unemployment insurance, isn't this a cost of the entry of illegals (U.S. Department of Justice, 1976)? This is hypothesis, not fact. One might equally logically argue that if illegals are not displacing national workers, and are contributing more financially than they are receiving in social services, then the illegals are in part financing the costs of the social services for unemployed or underemployed national workers.

Without trying to resolve these debating points, the crux of the argument comes back to the impact of illegal immigrants on the labor market. We think it is fair to state, on the basis of the evidence available, that one can take either view (that illegals seriously adversely affect nonskilled national workers, or that the illegals mostly take jobs nationals will not take), and support the view by partial statistics. The empirical evidence, we believe, is inadequate. Following are some additional arguments relevant to this theme.

According to the North and Houstoun study, 24 percent of the respondents in the sample were paid less than the minimum wage in their most recent job. The percentages were higher for domestic workers (almost two-thirds) and farmworkers (one-third). The lowest wages were paid to respondents who worked in the Southwest, where many of the Mexicans work. The study also reported what one might have anticipated, given the lower educational and skill levels of the Mexican as compared with illegals from many other areas, that the average hourly wage of the Mexican workers was the lowest among the illegals. The study also notes that respondents employed in the Southwest were two or three times more likely than respondents from other areas to report that they had been hired because they were illegals.

Illegal immigrants enter into all kinds of work. Those coming from areas other than Mexico and Latin America tend to enter the higher prestige and higher paying jobs (although often in a less prestigious occupation than in the home country, i.e., white collar workers often become blue collar workers in the United States), and the Mexicans tend to occupy low paying jobs in the secondary market (North and Houstoun, 1976). According to each of the three major study samples already cited (North and Houstoun, 1976; Villalpando et al., 1977; and Cornelius, 1976), a majority of Mexican illegals worked in agriculture or other occupations requiring minimum skills at the time of apprehension. It would appear that except for California and first employment on entering the United States, the proportion of illegals working in agriculture is declining. The argument inherent in the view of "leave well enough alone" regarding Mexican illegal immigrants is that they are filling jobs needed in modern societies which nationals do not want. As a woman ranchowner from south Texas contended in what is almost caricature: it is impossible to get anyone but illegals to clean the stables. Or, and this is a variant of this argument, many of the jobs are on the farms and the major unemployment problem in the United States is in the cities, among the youth and minorities. Or, and this is another argument, the "reservation price" of national workers, that price at which it would pay them to give up welfare, is higher than what the occupations into which the Mexicans go can legitimately demand (Reubens, 1978) without the jobs going out of existence or being replaced by labor-saving machinery, as has happened already in much of the country. It is either illegal workers or no workers, so why mess with what is working and serving a valuable purpose?

There is, of course, a converse argument, that what is true for household servants may not be true for all types of agriculture, and what is true for agriculture may not be true for construction, and so on into services, small industry, and the like (Briggs, 1975c). Just as jobs are differentiated, so too would there be a varied response by nationals to different kinds of job opportunities. Any government has a first obligation to its own nationals, else why the nation-state; and if our immigration system benefits the whole at even the partial expense of an underclass of minorities and youths, is this not reversing what should be the order of things?

It is precisely in this area where better knowledge is crucial. Edwin Reubens (1978) has noted that if the inflow of all aliens (legals, temporary workers, and illegals) adds one million persons per year, this is fully half of the annual growth of our reported labor force. What if the inflow figure is not one million, but double that? Is our economy capable of producing this many jobs in the secondary labor market to accommodate all comers? If the status of illegal aliens is regularized, will they remain in the secondary labor market?

We can summarize this option. The benefits of doing nothing are that the current system does provide needed labor, frequently below or at the minimum wage, for those who are most unskilled. This rewards them (since they are receiving more than they would at home) and U.S. society as a whole. It affords Mexico a safety valve for economic and political discontent by exporting part of its labor problem and enables Mexico to acquire a substantial number of dollars through remittances. The major cost is that the benefit to the majority is at the expense of the most disadvantaged minority (the unemployed and the lowest income groups) in our society (Briggs, 1974). We lack the facts to weigh the two considerations accurately. Our own view is that the benefit of the doubt should go to improving the lot of the most disadvantaged United States nationals; and if we are not prepared to accomplish this by seeking to curtail drastically the flow of illegal immigrants (we take it we are not and perhaps should not be), then the recompense must come in some other form. This is a common principle in economics, of the gainers compensating the losers and everybody coming out ahead. This is the concept behind adjustment assistance in foreign trade policy, under which workers and industries hurt by imports are given special aid. At the least, as a society, we owe more adjustment assistance (more training, more education, and other targeted programs of assistance) than we have been giving to the evident domestic losers from our immigration policy.

2. Legalize the Illegal

To be simplistic, the illegal aliens are illegal because the law says so. They would be legal if the law stated that. This approach is reminiscent of the observation of the Wickersham Commission during Prohibition that if one permitted the people to have alcohol, the problem of keeping them from it would be greatly simplified. There are many ways to accomplish this. The most frequently suggested is to have a program to admit Mexican workers on a temporary basis, comparable to the European contract labor programs. We will return to this suggestion. Another backdoor way of accomplishing this same result is to devise a Mexico Proviso imitative of the Texas Proviso: it would be illegal to cross the border into the United States from Mexico without documentation unless a job is found and the employer certifies that the migrant is working. There could be civil penalties for employers failing to make such reports. Further refinements might be that the employer must also certify that the work is temporary (say, no more than six to eight months) and that he is paying at least the minimum wage and other usual fringe benefits and is withholding the usual taxes. Other variants can be conceived.

There is nothing that makes the Mexican side of the border different from the United States side except as the nation-state has made it different. If one can look beyond that important but imposed difference, both areas have considerable history in common and much the same geography and topography. Both lack water, and many diseases cross back and forth without documentation. The prosperity of the Mexican side depends more on what is taking place on the United States side than what is happening elsewhere in Mexico (Urquidi, 1978). Many analysts decry the existence of the border industries in Mexico, the so-called *ma-*

quiladora, under which goods are partially manufactured in the United States, sent to Mexico for some additional labor-intensive processing, and then brought back into the United States under a duty levied only on the value added in Mexico (Bustamante, 1976*b*). Mexicans who object to the *maquiladora* system are concerned because it provides jobs for only some 90,000 Mexicans and does not have substantial linkages with the rest of the Mexican economy. They also suggest that assembly plants do not tend to be stable additions to the economy.

These industries, because of their proximity to the United States, have helped make the border region in Mexico a growth area. Population is increasing in this area faster than elsewhere in Mexico, save perhaps for Mexico City and other metropolitan centers; health services are better and wages are higher. The basis for the objection, in essence, is nationalism. Natural linkages with the United States are being exploited rather than more complicated and less natural linkages with distant points in Mexico. There is nothing that says an assembly industry must remain the only and final step in an industrialization process, as the critics of the *maquiladora* have asserted; there are enough examples of assembly leading to more sophisticated industry, as in Taiwan and South Korea, and this could happen in Mexico given policy stimulus to this end.

Our point is a straightforward one. Given their natural affinity, both sides of the border are more prosperous because of the heavy movement of people—100 million aliens crossed into the United States from Mexico in the year ended September 30, 1977 (INS,

1977*a*)—than they would be if there were sparse movement. Since cross-border movement occurs in any event, (goods travel legally under the *maquiladora*, and people travel clandestinely) why not make it all legal? This would also meet the age-old human aspiration to better one's lot by moving from one place to another.

The cost probably would be no more than the cost of the present system. The major impact, as under the current system, would be on the labor market. It is for this reason that our Mexico Proviso suggestion includes a minimum wage condition (whose enforcement obviously would not be simple), since this might reduce the demand for Mexicans as opposed to natives. It could save on the cost of border patrol, detention, and deportation, but this is marginal; and it would be cheaper than a new bureaucratically operated program of temporary work permits.

We do not know if this option, of open borders with certification at the temporary job end, is politically feasible. We suspect it is not. We do not know whether removal of the stigma of the word "illegal" (Cornelius argues that going across the border without papers is so common that the word illegal is almost a badge of pride) would lead to a quantum jump in the number of Mexicans coming to the United States to look for work. However, the option has attractions (Gordon, 1975). It removes the inherent dishonesty of our current system; it responds to stated employer needs in the United States, save possibly for the minimum wage requirement; and it would recognize the reality of economic interdependence. This legalization-certification system could be confined to migrants coming from Mexico, if we wished, on the grounds of contiguity. At a minimum, it is worth considering.

3. *Seek to Close the Border More Tightly*

This is the third in the natural trio of broad options: do nothing; open the border; close the border. The ultimate logic of the nation-state would lead to this third option. It is what most other countries do. In Switzerland, for example, the border was opened for temporary workers when they were needed, and with the recent economic slowdown, the Swiss passed a law that no Swiss national can be fired unless temporary alien workers already have been laid off. Jonathan Power, writing in *The Washington Post* (Power, 1978), called this the policy of the lemon; first squeeze the fruit and then throw it away. The big difference between the United States and European countries is the U.S.'s long, sparsely controlled border. Immigration problems are due, not just to income disparities, but to the combination of income disparities and contiguity. Using 1977 World Bank data, the per capita GNP relationship between the United States and Mexico was 7.9 to 1, compared to, say Switzerland/Turkey of 9.0 to 1 and France/Algeria of 6.6 to 1. (In all the sending countries, the average per capita GNP really says little about the income of the migrant, but the relationship between the migrant's income and the average is probably comparable in all of them.)

If we decided to do so, we probably could close the border more tightly. It would take money, more sensing and related equipment, more personnel, but this would be a matter of resource use. To call this a Berlin

Wall (which is designed to keep people from leaving) would be an exaggeration; it need not be different from entry into Switzerland or the Netherlands from the outside. It would not be perfect—many people would slip through—but it is hard to believe that if we wished, we could not slow the process of illegal entry. The price would be financial (the cost of closing the border); economic (possible slower United States growth by closing off natural interdependence); and mostly psychological (we would stop being a country of relatively open borders). The consequence of this choice, if we mean to cut off illegal immigrants working in the United States, is that not only would the border be more tightly closed, but also that there would be more roundup drives against illegals throughout the country. This, in turn, implies a better system of identification for all persons to make these roundups effective. The Europeans generally do have identification card systems.

A unilateral closing of the border by the United States obviously would have repercussions on political relations with Mexico, and Mexico could face a difficult internal problem if its emigration safety valve were closed (Bustamante, 1978a). Yet, some border closing was implicit in the president's proposal and may be necessary in an expanded system of work permits. Amnesty is not intended to be a perpetual process. Letting some in with work permits and letting others in without permits, each to go his or her own way in the labor market, hardly makes sense. To overcome this logical problem, and to acknowledge rhetorically the costs of the border closure, the United

States government uses less drastic language; it refers to "substantial increases of enforcement resources" (U.S. Department of Justice, 1978) to control the southern border.

Our prediction is that we will end up with a game of chicken. We will increase border vigilance and the illegal immigrants will become more sophisticated in their elusive techniques; the result is likely to be a stalemate at a higher cost in years ahead. If we wish to be effective in "sealing" the border, then it probably must be done the way the Europeans do, with all the accompanying inland paraphernalia as well; and we do not know if this is the will of the political majority.

Rather than trying to close the border unilaterally, another approach would be binational cooperation, with Mexico playing a major role in controlling or regulating the flow in return for identifiable benefits. We will return to this idea.

4. Punish the Employers

If we do not wish to bear the cost of closing the border more tightly, that is, if we are unprepared to deal with the supply of illegal immigrants, then an alternative is to reduce the demand for them. The idea of punishing employers who knowingly hire illegals is directed to this end. Representative Rodino of New Jersey has been proposing this for years with no result, and President Carter has picked up the idea. It is well known that in order to punish employers, some basis is needed to prove that an employer "knowingly" hired an illegal. The best way to do this is with an identity card or a universal work permit. The violations of our civil liberties practiced by the FBI and the CIA which have become apparent in recent years must have influenced the president's decision not to propose a universal identity card. Certainly he was influenced by the expressed concerns of Mexican-American and civil liberty groups. The administration's compromise proposal was to use a more forgery-proof social security card and other documentation not precisely specified, as evidence of legal status. Employers would be punished by civil action (injunctive relief and a maximum fine of $1,000 for each undocumented alien), but only if it could be shown that the employer followed a "pattern or practice" of hiring illegals. There is no need to rehearse again the potential benefits and costs of this option on the labor market, and on production in various sectors of the economy, since they are comparable to those already discussed. There has been some opposition to this proposal on the grounds that it will not work, that employers will continue to hire illegals since the gains from hiring will exceed the costs of getting caught (Cornelius, 1977b), but this really depends on the hiring exceptions provided in the law and the rigor of the enforcement.

The main opposition to the employer sanction is just the reverse, that it will work too well. To use the words of the Mexican American Legal Defense Educational Fund (1977), "its adoption would unavoidably lead to widespread employment discrimination against ethnic Americans in general, and Mexican Americans in particular. Faced with a statute making it illegal to hire undocumented workers, some employers would be overzealous in their actions, and would refuse to hire anyone whom they suspected of unlawful entry, however unfounded the suspicion and regardless of the proof of legal residence provided."

Living in the Southwest, and having many Americans of Mexican origin among our friends, colleagues, and students, we have become impressed with the emotional scars many of them bear due to overt discrimination and perpetual insults. They know, for instance, that the border patrol will stop only cars with Hispanic-looking occupants, will shove in a flashlight, and ask for documents in their search of illegals. The recent evidence of police discrimination in the Southwest against Mexican-Americans is merely the newspaper headline manifestation of a long-simmering pattern of prejudice. Demanding that all job seekers show documentary proof of legality would not overcome this problem, or so MALDEF and other Mexican-American groups are convinced, since the employer would still focus on the Hispanics.

If the supply of illegals is not closed at the border and inland, and if demand is not diminished at the hiring end, then there really is no way to keep the illegal immigrants out. This is the ineluctable logic of the MALDEF position and that of other organized Mexican-American groups.

5. *Expand the System of Temporary Worker Visas*

Many authorities on this subject have advocated variants of an expanded permit system for temporary workers. The administration decided against this. President Carter, in a press conference on May 12, 1978, with representatives from the Hispanic media, stated explicitly: "We made it clear when we sent up the legislation to Congress that we don't intend to expand the H-2 program or to put in any sort of *bracero* program." Under the H-2 program visas are issued for temporary workers for specific employer needs, for instance at harvest time. In U.S. fiscal year 1976, about 25,000 certifications were granted for temporary workers, 15,000 in activities related to agriculture and 10,000 in nonagricultural industries, services, and professions (Marshall, 1978*a*).

The movement of workers across the border is deeply rooted historically dating back to the demands for labor generated by the mining booms and railroad construction in the last century and by the requirements of agriculture in the present one. However, it was during the manpower shortages of the First World War that the movement assumed significant dimensions. The inward flow continued until the depression of the thirties when, between 1930 and 1933, over 300,000 Mexicans were repatriated to Mexico (Carreras de Velasco, 1974). The human tide reversed again during World War II. As a result of new manpower shortages, the *bracero* program was inaugurated in 1942 as a wartime measure. It was to endure much longer than anticipated.

The *bracero* program lasted for 22 years and under its auspices some four and a half million Mexican workers labored under contract for limited periods of time. They never were found on more than 2 percent of U.S. farms, and these were highly concentrated in the Southwest and California. The program always was the object of political skirmishes and was and remains a controversial subject (Craig, 1971; Galarza, 1964). Contemporary complaints and later research revealed much graft and exploitation in carrying it out. A number of interesting facts can be gleaned from this historical experience in contract labor. Mexico, in addition to insisting on additional protection for its nationals with each renegotiation, demonstrated a preference for intergovernmental agreements. By the early 1950s, it is estimated that the *braceros* and illegal workers in the United States were remitting more than $100 million annually. By 1952 the *bracero* program had been "institutionalized" and had become a "permanent" component of United States farm labor and of United States–Mexican relations.

In the negotiations Mexico advocated a government-sponsored system to oversee the contracting, which was established; and punishment of employers of illegals, which was not forthcoming. At the time *both* delegations pledged "a redoubling of efforts on the part of their respective immigration authorities to prevent illegal entry." Much criticism was heard about the fact that a rising number of apprehensions of illegal migrants accompanied the *bracero* program. Apprehensions ran two to four times the number of *braceros* in a given year between 1948 and 1954. These statistics, when added to the post–Korean War economic slowdown, brought "Operation Wetback," under which a militarized border patrol rounded up and deported over a million aliens—men, women, and children—in 1954. By 1956, apprehensions had dropped to 73,000 and the INS could report that illegal crossing was under control; the price in violation of human rights was high. The year 1956 also happened to be a peak for *braceros*; 445,000 entered the United States that year (Craig, 1971).

During these years political agitation against the program increased, and the *bracero* arrangement would have been ended in 1961 except for Mexican advocacy of prolongation and domestic pressure to avoid an abrupt termination. As a concession to those pressures the Kennedy administration continued the arrangement until 1964, when it was allowed to expire (Craig, 1971). Apart from corruption and exploitation, the biggest complaint was that the *bracero* program was accompanied by significant illegal entry. There is also more recent evidence that those who learned the ropes as *braceros*—or their offspring—became the cadre for the later illegals. Despite this history, many Mexicans and Americans have argued that legal contracts, in industry as well as agriculture, are more likely to produce equitable treatment of alien workers than the absence of any contract; and that by legalizing some workers, a good case can be made for securing Mexican cooperation to close the border to others while still meeting the employer needs in the United States. The administration opposition to temporary contract labor is based primarily on labor union opposition. The Justice Department also makes another argument, that a *bracero*-like program involves an indentured type of employment which "weakens our free enterprise system." To counter this argument, Cornelius (1978*a*) has suggested that the temporary visa not bind the worker to any particular employer. The control he advocates is a requirement that the worker leave the country for at least six months a year. It is not clear how to assure that the temporary workers will indeed leave. (Even in Europe, where it is harder to blend into the society, many do not leave, or not immediately, or shortly thereafter reenter the country.)

There is obviously attraction to legalizing what will take place in any event, particularly if one believes that the workers are needed. This would give both United States and Mexican authorities some basis to monitor treatment of the workers. The flaw in the idea, as already indicated, is that legalizing some temporary workers will not keep out others, unless these admitted legally are as numerous as those now coming illegally. The system will work only if control of the border is tightened, or employers are severely fined for hiring migrants without temporary work visas.

The second problem with the proposal relates to United States politics. How many temporary workers are needed, a hundred thousand, a million, more? If the labor unions consented to a contract work program (either job-specific or general, although we suspect that a general program would be less politically palatable), the negotiation would then center on numbers. It is hard to believe that the number of legals that would be permitted would reach whatever the current number is of illegals. If the number of permitted or legalized workers were too small, then this option would affect only a small part of the problem.

6. *Amnesty*

We wish merely to touch on the amnesty issue and not analyze its merits or demerits since it is a humanitarian gesture and not a proposal to help solve the future illegal migration issue, nor can it do so. Most analysts would agree, we think, that amnesty by itself would exacerbate the migration problem by giving still another inducement for illegals to stay here if they are so inclined. Amnesty for those who have been here for years, put down roots, and developed a stake in our system, under the formula the president has proposed, or a more liberal version (making the cutoff date for permanent resident status later, say January 1, 1977, instead of January 1, 1970, as MALDEF has proposed) implies that other measures of the type we have discussed here will be used either to limit the future supply of illegal aliens or the demand for them.

7. *Other United States Actions*

For the sake of completeness, we should note that various other actions by the United States were contemplated in the president's program (Carter, 1977). One existing irritant resulted from the recent imposition of a 20,000 ceiling on legal migration from any single Western Hemisphere country. Before that restriction was approved, legal migration from Mexico had reached a peak annual figure of 70,000 (*New York Times*, 1976). President Carter accepted a proposal to combine the Mexican and Canadian immigration quotas and raise the total from 40,000 to 50,000, thereby increasing the availability of immigration visas for Mexicans. He also recommended strengthening the visa-issuing function of the State Department to minimize visa fraud and improving administration of the Fair Labor Standards and the Federal Farm Labor

Contractor Registration Acts. These actions have merit in their own right, but they are peripheral to the central issue of dealing with illegal immigrants from Mexico. Most Mexican illegals enter without documentation, so that improved visa-issuing techniques will hardly affect them. If illegal entrants number in the hundreds of thousands or millions, raising the Mexican immigration quota from 20,000 a year to 50,000 a year for Mexico and Canada combined will not be statistically significant. As the administration admitted, better enforcement of existing laws will still not make it illegal for an employer to hire a worker who is illegally in the United States.

The administration also proposed to make it a criminal offense to receive pay for knowingly assisting an undocumented alien to obtain or retain a job. This is aimed at the so-called *polleros* or *coyotes* who help illegals get across the border and find a job. If crime pays, there unquestionably will be practitioners.

IV. Treat the Cause and Not the Symptoms

IT IS GENERALLY ACCEPTED that Mexicans migrate illegally to the United States because of lack of opportunity and low earnings at home compared with attractive work opportunities in the United States. Most illegal immigrants have no difficulty getting work in the United States. At an average hourly wage of $2.34 (the figure for the Mexicans in the North and Houstoun sample of May–June 1975), the illegals are well paid by their national standard. Study after study reveals that the overwhelmingly dominant motive for Mexican migration is economic. If this incentive can be reduced through Mexican development and job creation, this, the argument goes, is the way to solve the migration problem. To cite MALDEF: "The principal focus of any proposal to reduce undocumented immigration should be upon elimination of conditions in source countries prompting such immigration." No one can really quarrel with the thesis that it would be nice if the factors pushing Mexicans to leave did not exist, or that, to bring this about, the United States should do what it can to help Mexico develop economically, but Keynes' famous commentary about the long run as a policy guide is most appropriate here. As he put it: "Economists set themselves too easy, too useless a task if in tempestuous seasons they can only tell us that when the storm is long past the ocean is flat again."

It is hard to know precisely what the advocates of dealing with the cause and not the symptoms wish us to do. Apparently most have in mind nonconcessionary development assistance aimed at providing expanded economic opportunities through the initiation of labor-intensive activities. However, the cumulative value of Mexico's loans from the World Bank as of June 30, 1977 amounted to $2.8 billion and from the Inter-American Development Bank (IDB) as of December 31, 1977 to $1.6 billion. Among the clients of the World Bank's regular window and all IDB windows combined, Mexico ranks second to Brazil in the value of loans received; it ranks lower per capita, but still quite high. Looking to the future, because of Mexican oil and natural gas discoveries, it is unlikely that the balance of payments or the lack of absorbable financial resources will be constraints on Mexican growth. Further loans from us, either directly (which Mexico does not favor) or through international institutions, would likely be redundant. Mexico did not react favorably to various trial balloons floated by United States legislators that a special United States–Mexican development loan fund be established to help create jobs in Mexico. United States Ambassador Lucey publicly reported that there was little Mexican interest in direct United States development assistance. A shortage of funds almost certainly will not be the problem.

The causes of Mexican emigration lie deep within

Mexican society. Mexico's population growth rate until recently was about 3.5 percent a year, one of the highest growth rates in the world. It may have come down to 3.0 percent, which is still extremely high. The Latin American Demography Center estimated that Mexico's population will increase from 59 million in 1975 to 83 million in 1985, to 132 million in the year 2000. Combined unemployment and underemployment now must affect about 40 percent of the population, although there are no precise figures for this (Urquidi and Villarreal, 1978). In his inaugural address in December 1976, President López Portillo stated that the unemployment rate was 26 percent and that the percentage of underemployed was even higher (López Portillo, 1976). The number of persons entering Mexico's labor force each year (defined by Mexico as those reaching age 12) is about 650,000. Despite Mexico's high growth rate in recent decades (2.8 percent per capita per year from 1960 to 1975), the country has been unable to absorb this level of population growth. Even if the slowed rate of population growth reported by researchers at El Colegio de México proves correct (Riding, 1977), the hundredth million Mexican is already on the way and the projection for the end of the century would be reduced only to 115 million. Worse still from the viewpoint of labor absorption, particularly as one looks ahead, is the extreme youthfulness of the Mexican population with almost half under the age of fifteen.

Interdependence means there is a flow of people to the nearest place of reasonable opportunity, to Mexico City, to other Mexican urban centers, to the northern border, and over the border. The famous nineteenth-century Mexican statement can legitimately be reversed: poor United States, so close to Mexico.

Despite the historical fact that Mexico was the locale of the first twentieth-century nationalist social revolution, it remains one of the more unequal societies in Latin America and among the world's middle-income countries. The seeming contradiction results from inequitable distribution of income and wealth created by Mexico's economic progress. Using data from a Bank of Mexico survey, the richest 5 percent of the population received 36 percent of total income in 1969, the richest 20 percent received 64 percent, and by contrast, the poorest 20 percent received 4 percent (Banco de México, 1974). Evidence from the mid-seventies from the Bank of Mexico shows little change and possibly deterioration in the share of the lowest 10 and 20 percent (Banco de México, 1977). Mexico's average GNP is reasonably high by world standards (over $1000 per person per year), but a good proportion of the population does not share in this. This, too, drives people over the border. This distributional inequality is not curable by foreign financial help.

As one looks at Mexican growth over recent decades, one is struck by the relative growth of industry and services and the relative decline in agriculture. From 1950 to 1975, the contribution of manufacturing to Mexico's gross domestic product rose from 18 to 23 percent, that of services remained relatively constant at 55–56 percent, and that of agriculture and livestock declined from 16 to 9 percent. This phenomenon is not unnatural for countries with high growth rates.

However, it has meant an exodus from rural to urban areas, and from both out of Mexico, because of the lack of job opportunities in the urban areas. In 1950, by its definition, Mexico was 57 percent rural and 43 percent urban; by 1976 the figures were 37 percent rural and 63 percent urban. This has led some to suggest that the United States should help Mexico keep 'em down on the farm, or at least in rural areas. Indeed, some effort to do this is underway with the help of World Bank loans directed not only at large-scale agriculture, but at smaller-scale farming. Perhaps the exodus from rural areas can be slowed, but even this is questionable. Raúl Prebisch, the distinguished Latin American political economist, pointed out in a study in 1970 for the Inter-American Development Bank that "the exodus of agricultural workers is inevitable if the level of the rural masses is to be raised" (Prebisch, 1970). He was discussing Latin America generally, but the same holds true for Mexico, as it did for the United States, Europe, Japan, and elsewhere. It would be chimerical to look towards keeping Mexicans on the farms or in rural areas as a cure for the migration disease.

Different versions of precisely this solution have been suggested. Jorge Bustamante (1978*b*), of El Colegio de México, who has written extensively on the migration problem, has suggested setting up collectives or cooperatives not far from the border where fruits and vegetables could be produced and processed for sale in the United States as one way of keeping Mexicans at home. Cornelius (1978*a*) has advocated setting up nonagricultural employment opportunities in rural

areas (such as textiles, shoes, and furniture manufacturing). This does not differ markedly from *maquiladora*, except for the source of capital and the potential
completeness of the manufacturing process. The un-
fortunate fact is that it is difficult to set up industrial
centers away from population centers where the sup-
pliers and markets, as well as the skills, exist. It has
been done, but it also has failed time and time again.
Remember that the existing *maquiladoras* at peak provided employment for 90,000 workers and the current
Alliance for Production launched by President López
Portillo called for the creation of 150,000 more positions (López Portillo, 1976). How many plants would it
take, over what time period, to employ a million people in this way? Where would the products go? Bustamante proposes a five-year period of special access to
the United States market for the production of such
enterprises (Bustamante, 1978*b*).

Mexicans sometimes assert that United States trade
policy results in importing Mexican people instead of
Mexican goods. There is something to this: the United
States maintains import restrictions on Mexican textiles and other products, and high duties on some
Mexican vegetables, but quantitatively the restrictions cannot really affect the employment of more than
a few thousand people. More precise data would be
useful. The problem could get worse if Mexico were
as successful a producer of consumer goods as Hong
Kong, Taiwan, and South Korea are, but this is a the-
oretical possibility rather than a cause of current illegal migration.

By all means, Mexico must treat the causes of its own

unemployment and distributional problems, and the United States has an obligation to help in this process, for instance by minimizing import restrictions; but this is a long-haul process and will not get us through the current tempest.

There is a reverse side to American obligation to Mexico. Mexico also has an obligation to cooperate with the United States in dealing currently with the problem of illegal migration. It is true that the United States can be said to have caused the problem by being there and creating the pull that brings the migrants. It is much more to the point to state that Mexico has created the problem by its internal social and economic conditions. Bustamante (1976c) has referred to the two-sidedness of the problem, the U.S. demand for cheap labor as he put it, and the underdevelopment and population trends in Mexico; he concluded that any realistic solution must emerge from a binational approach. He does not specify what the Mexican contribution should be to this approach.

If we assume that a binational approach should involve some form of contract labor from Mexico, this, as already noted, implies some effort either to limit the supply of noncontracted workers or the demand for them. Amnesty requires a future limitation of illegals. Would Mexico be able to limit the exodus of its own illegals on the grounds of lack of proper documentation? Many countries limit exit (or reentry) to persons with valid visas or other entry permits to their country of destination. At the outset of any discussion Mexicans automatically raise the issue posed by their compatriots' constitutional right to freedom of movement. The argument is suggestive and prompts our guess that no Mexican government is prepared politically to limit the flow, or would want to do so. However, if the number contracted for were large enough to release the pent-up internal pressure, then it might be possible to secure some Mexican cooperation. It is possible that a bilateral agreement, with appropriate *quid pro quos*, might bring a search for ways to cooperate.

This is another of the vexing features of this issue. We are convinced that an effective program to contain the flow of illegals while at the same time maintaining United States–Mexican cordiality, requires a cooperative effort, and yet we doubt that Mexico is able to carry out its part of the effort. Except for dictatorial regimes, such as those in the Communist countries, it is hard to keep people from leaving. Yet, if the supply is to be curtailed, it would be immensely helpful if Mexico did its share to regulate the flow.

V. Conclusions

THERE IS NO GOOD WAY to solve the problem of illegal migrants from Mexico. We deal in this area with degrees of unsatisfactoriness. This is compounded by uncertainty about the underlying facts and, hence, of the economic and labor market impact of the flow of persons into the United States. We wish to preserve good relations with Mexico, which we believe means not shutting off the safety valve, at least not abruptly. Were the flow of illegals to be completely stanched, many producers on this side of the border would be hurt (and some persons in the secondary labor market would be helped), but the United States could adjust calmly, at a lower level of national production, to the new labor situation. Mexico, over time, would adjust as well, but possibly only after some turbulence.

As in all complex issues, policymaking involves tradeoffs. In this case, the main ones are: (1) damaging some United States workers by the present migration pattern versus benefitting the total United States economy by having workers from Mexico; (2) carrying out the law (either by more effective border closure, the use of some identification document in order to punish employers of illegal aliens, or both) versus threatening civil liberties; and (3) basing policy solely on the perceived domestic political and economic consequences of our actions versus partially subordinating these to take into account the ramifications in Mexico of what we do. Making choices is immensely complicated by our ignorance of many underlying facts. Our policy suggestions are based on choices between competing interests. We believe that the availability of Mexican workers helps more than it hurts the United States economy; we believe that it is important to the fabric of United States society to carry out its laws; and we believe that policy must be based on the mutuality of United States and Mexican needs. The interagency study by the United States government of United States–Mexican relations preceding President Carter's visit to Mexico in February 1979 included the immigration problem as one of its major concerns.

Where does this ordering of priorities lead us? Because of the contribution the illegals make to the United States economy, our major recommendation is precisely the reverse of the president's. We believe that a significant labor program should be instituted under which visas for temporary work, say, for no more than six to eight months a year, would be given to hundreds of thousands of Mexicans. How many hundreds of thousands can be determined after surveying the United States as to the demand, both in industry and agriculture. There could be agreement at the outset that the number to be admitted would progressively decline over a definite timetable (although we might regret this if projections of shortages in the United States supply of workers in the secondary labor market materialized).

We are under no illusions and realize that this would

conjure up fears of another *bracero* program, accompanied by graft at the sending end and exploitation at the receiving end, but these things occur even more blatantly now without any intervention of the authorities. We realize that most labor unions will oppose this policy recommendation because of the labor market impact, but, again, what we propose is preferable to the current situation. We recognize that many of the "temporary" workers would become permanent, as they married and had children and either went underground or sought a change of status, but the majority should go home to return again another year. We assume that the demand for such contract labor would be made known at the local level for certification at the federal level. This can be called indenture, but it is indenture with some possibility of supervision by two governments, for temporary periods, and with more rights for the workers than they now enjoy in their illegal freedom. This may be only marginal improvement, but it is improvement.

The labor market impact of a temporary worker program which obligated the employer to pay the minimum wage and the current fringe benefits would be less than the impact of the present system. Nevertheless, such a program would require compensatory benefits to those most likely to be adversely affected. A corollary of temporary work visas is an obligation of the localities and the federal government jointly to augment programs for affected United States workers.

To borrow a phrase, you can't do just one thing. More legal temporary work visas, if they are to really limit the number of migrants, requires dealing with either the demand or supply of noncontracted workers. The most straightforward way to do this is to make it more difficult to cross the border into the United States without documentation. If the Mexican government is prepared to cooperate, then we recommend a tighter seal on our side of the border. Failing this cooperation, since we doubt that Mexico could control exit of its nationals, we would reluctantly advise civil sanctions against hiring illegals, with all the supporting paraphernalia this implies, as in the administration's proposal. Employers would have less cause to complain under these recommendations than under the administration's since they would have the option of hiring Mexicans with work permits, albeit for temporary periods and at the minimum wage.

The concerns of the Mexican-American community that improved social security cards or other forms of identification will lead to job discrimination against Hispanics is harder to deal with, since it is an anticipatory and emotional fear. The fact that employers will be hiring Mexicans in any event under this set of recommendations should have some ameliorating effect about concern over prejudice. However, if this proposal turns out not to be acceptable, then the only significant option left is to do nothing. But since the flow of migrants will inevitably increase, and consequently the economic and political pressures to do something about it, doing nothing means postponing confronting an issue that is likely to worsen.

However, without an expanded temporary visa system, accompanied by supply or demand limitations on nonvisaed migrants and the necessary measures to make these limitations effective, we would recommend maintaining the status quo. The current system is more cruel than a system of temporary work permits, since an illegal immigrant has no rights after he or she is squeezed, whereas a person legally admitted to the United States would have rights. However, the current system does benefit many Mexicans and many more Americans than are hurt by it; and it should not be abandoned by the sort of cold-turkey attempt to cut off demand for migrants (by punishing employers) or supply (by reinforcing the border patrol) that was contemplated in the administration's proposal. Cooperative relations with Mexico require that its safety valve not be closed abruptly, but that time for adjustment be given.

In summary, we advocate a program which includes the following elements:

1. Adjustment of status for those who have acquired a stake in our society;
2. A significant contract labor program declining on a preagreed time schedule;
3. A cooperative binational effort to regulate the movement of migrants in order to minimize the number of illegals entering the United States.

References

Alba, Francisco. 1978. "Industrialización sustitutiva y migración internacional: El caso de México." *Foro Internacional* 18 (3): 464–479 (January–March).

Arellano, Richard G. 1977. "Department Testifies on Undocumented Aliens: Statement, September 14, 1977." *Department of State Bulletin* 77: 592–594 (October).

Austin American Statesman. 1977. "Alien Bill Passage Predicted" (October 14).

Banco de México. 1974. *La distribución del ingreso en México, 1968*. Mexico City: Fondo de Cultura Económica.

———. 1977. *Encuesta de ingresos y gastos familiares, 1975*. Mexico City: Centro de Información y Estadísticas del Trabajo.

Blum, Bill. 1978. "Targeting the Illegal Alien." *Inquiry*, July 24, pp. 20–23.

Briggs, Vernon M., Jr. 1974. *The Mexico–United States Border: Public Policy and Chicano Economic Welfare*. Austin: Center for the Study of Human Resources and the Bureau of Business Research, the University of Texas (June).

———. 1975a. "Mexican Workers in the United States Labour Market: A Contemporary Dilemma." *International Labour Review* 112(5): 351–368 (November).

———. 1975b. "Illegal Aliens: The Need for a More Restrictive Border Policy." *Social Science Quarterly* 56(3): 477–484 (December).

———. 1975c. "Mexican Migration and the U.S. Labor Market: A Mounting Issue for the Seventies." Based on a conference paper. Austin: Center for the Study of Human Resources and the Bureau of Business Research, the University of Texas.

———. 1976. "Illegal Immigration and the American Labor Force: The Use of Soft Data for Analysis." *American Behavioral Science* 19:351–363 (January).

———. 1977. "The Problem of Illegal Immigration [United States]." *Texas Business Review* 51:171–175 (August).

Bustamante, Jorge. 1976*a*. "Structural and Ideological Conditions of the Mexican Undocumented Immigration to the United States [Bibliography]." *American Behavioral Science* 19:364–376 (January).

———. 1976*b*. "Maquiladoras: A New Face of International Capitalism in Mexico's Northern Frontier." Paper prepared for the Latin American Studies Association, Atlanta, Georgia (March). [Processed.]

———. 1976*c*. "The Silent Invasion Issue." Paper prepared for Population Association of America, Montreal, Canada (April). [Processed.]

———. 1978*a*. "Comentarios: Las propuestas de política migratoria en los Estados Unidos y sus repercusiones en México." *Foro Internacional* 18(3):522–530 (January–March).

———. 1978*b*. "Emigración indocumentada a los Estados Unidos." *Foro Internacional* 18(3):430–463 (January–March).

———. 1978*c*. "Commodity-Migrants: Structural Analysis of Mexican Immigration to the United States." In *Views across the Border: The United States and Mexico*, ed. Stanley R. Ross, pp. 193–203. Albuquerque: University of New Mexico Press.

Cárdenas, Gilberto. 1976. "Public Data on Mexican Immigration into the United States: A Critical Evaluation." In *Current Issues in Social Policies*, ed. W. B. Litrell and C. S. Sjoberg. Beverly Hills: Sage Publishers.

Carreras de Velasco, Mercedes. 1974. *Los mexicanos que devolvió la crisis, 1929–1932*. Colección del Archivo Histórico Diplomático Mexicano, Tercera Época, 2. Mexico City: Secretaría de Relaciones Exteriores.

Carter, Jimmy. 1977. "Undocumented Aliens: Remarks and Message to Congress, August 4, 1977." *Department of State Bulletin* 77:315–320 (September 5).

Center Magazine. 1977. "Mexico—The Special Case [dialogue]." 10:67–80 (July).

Chapman, Stephen. 1977. "Let the Aliens In." *Washington Monthly*, July–August.

Congressional Digest. 1977. "Controversy over Proposed Amnesty for Illegal Aliens: Pro and Con." 56:225–256 (October).

Cornelius, Wayne. 1976. *Mexican Migration to the United States: The View from Rural Sending Communities.* Cambridge, Mass.: Migration and Development Study Group, Massachusetts Institute of Technology (June).

———. 1977a. "When the Door Is Closed to Illegal Aliens, Who Pays?" *New York Times*, June 1. Reprinted in *Immigration and Public Policy: Human Rights for Undocumented Workers and Their Families*, ed. Antonio José Ríos-Bustamante, pp. 105–106. Los Angeles: University of California at Los Angeles, Chicano Studies Center Document #5.

———. 1977b. "A Critique of the Carter Administration's Policy Proposals on Illegal Immigration." Presentation to the Carnegie Endowment for International Peace, "Face-to-Face" Seminar, Washington, D.C. (August 10).

———. 1978a. "La migración ilegal mexicana a los Estados Unidos: Conclusiones de investigaciones recientes, implicaciones políticas y prioridades de investigación." *Foro Internacional* 18(3):399–429 (January–March).

———. 1978b. *Mexican Migration to the United States: Causes, Consequences, and U.S. Responses.* Cambridge, Mass.: Migration and Development Study Group, Center for International Studies, Massachusetts Institute of Technology (July).

Craig, Richard B. 1971. *The Bracero Program: Interest Groups and Foreign Policy.* Austin: University of Texas Press.

Dallas Times Herald. 1977. "Mexican Workers Harvesting Crops in Texas Spark 'Bracero' Charges" (June 22), p. 10-A.

Del Olmo, Frank. 1977. "Guest Workers' Proposal Defended." *Los Angeles Times* (May 28). Reprinted in *Immigration and Public Policy: Human Rights for Undocumented Workers and Their Families*, ed. Antonio José Ríos-Bustamante, p. 103. Los Angeles: University of California at

Los Angeles, Chicano Studies Center Document #5.

Echeverría, Luis. 1976. "Sexto informe del gobierno que rinde al H. Congreso de la Unión Luis Echeverría, Presidente Constitucional, 1° de septiembre de 1976." *Excélsior* (September 2), p. 33-A:4.

Excélsior. 1978. "Son braceros 25% de los trabajadores mexicanos" (June 1), p. 11-A.

Fogel, Walter A. 1975. "Immigrant Mexicans and the U.S. Work Force." *Monthly Labor Review* 98:44–46 (May).

———. 1977a. "Major Changes to Control Immigration Flow." *Center Magazine* 10:46–47 (March).

———. 1977b. "Illegal Alien Workers in the United States." *Industrial Relations* 16:243–263 (October).

Frisbie, Peter. 1975. "Illegal Migration from Mexico to the United States: A Longitudinal Analysis." *International Migration Review* 9(1):3–13 (Spring).

Fullerton, Howard N., Jr., and Paul O. Flaim. 1977. *New Labor Force Projections to 1990.* Washington, D.C.: Bureau of Labor Statistics. Reprinted from *Monthly Labor Review* (December 1976).

Galarza, Ernesto. 1964. *Merchants of Labor: The Mexican Bracero History.* Santa Barbara, Calif.: McNally and Loftin.

Gallup Opinion Index. 1977. "Majority Would Prosecute Those Who Hire Illegal Aliens" (June), pp. 24–28.

Gándara, Arturo. 1978. "Chicanos y extrangeros ilegales: La conjunctión de sus derechos constitucionales frente el estado norteamericano." *Foro Internacional* 18(3):480–493 (January–March).

García y Griego, Manuel. 1978. "La polémica sobre el volumen de la emigración a Estados Unidos." In *Simposio sobre la emigración indocumentada mexicana a los Estados Unidos: Problemática general y soluciones alternativas.* Mexico: El Colegio de México (April 3).

Gordon, Wendell. 1975. "A Case for a Less Restrictive Border Policy." *Social Science Quarterly* 56(3):485–491 (December).

Graham, Otis L., Jr. 1977. "Illegal Immigration." *Center Magazine* 10:56–66 (July).

Grennes, Ron. 1977. Presentation at Conference on Immigration and the Mexican National, Trinity University, San Antonio, November 11–12.

Halsell, Grace. 1978. *The Illegals*. New York: Stein and Day.

Hansen, Niles. 1973. *Location Preferences, Migration and Regional Growth*. New York: Praeger.

———. 1978. "Alien Migration: A Comparative Study of Mexican Workers in the United States and European Guest Worker Experience." *Texas Business Review* (Bureau of Business Research, University of Texas at Austin) 52(6):107–111 (June).

Hohl, Donald G. 1977. "The Catholic Church Reacts to Carter's Proposal on the Undocumented Alien." *Agenda* 7(6):17–20 (November–December).

Immigration and Naturalization Service. 1976a. *Residential Survey of Illegal Aliens: Objective, Overview, Glossary*. Washington, D.C. (December).

———. 1976b. *Illegal Alien Study, Part 1: Fraudulent Entrants Study*. Washington, D.C.

———. 1977a. "Aliens and Citizens Admitted at United States Ports of Entry." Washington, D.C. (Year Ended September 30).

———. 1977b. "Monthly Report of Deportable Aliens Found in U.S. by Nationality, Status at Entry, Place of Entry, Status When Found" (Fiscal Year). Washington, D.C.

———. 1977c. *1976 Annual Report*. Washington, D.C.

———. 1977d. *Report on Apprehensions*. Washington, D.C.

———. 1977e. Office of Planning and Evaluation. *Perspectives on Immigration Policy: A Framework for Policy Analysis*. Washington, D.C. *Inter-American Economic Affairs*. 1976. "On the Problem of Illegal Mexican Aliens: Excerpts from the Comptroller-General's Report to the Congress Entitled: Immigration: Need to Reassess U.S. Policy." 30:93–96 (Winter).

———. 1977. "Data on the Illegal Aliens Problem." 31:95–96 (Summer).

Knapp, Charles B., Department of Labor. 1977. "Developing a National Policy to Deal with Undocumented Aliens." Paper for presentation at the Thirteenth Annual Winter Meeting of the Industrial Relations Research Association, New York City, December 28–30.

Lesko Associates. 1975. *Final Report: Basic Data and Guidance Required to Implement a Major Illegal Alien Study during Fiscal Year 1976*. Prepared for the Immigration and Naturalization Service (October).

López Portillo, José. 1976. "Discurso inaugural." *Excélsior* (December 2), p. 35-A.

———. 1977. "Primer informe de gobierno que rinde al H. Congreso de la Unión José López Portillo, Presidente Constitucional, 1° de septiembre de 1977." *Excélsior* (September 2).

McWilliams, Carey. 1977. "No Trespassing: What Became of the Land of Opportunity." *Skeptic* 20:49–53 (July–August).

Marshall, F. Ray. 1978a. Statement before the Committee on the Judiciary, United States Senate (May 11).

———. 1978b. "Economic Factors Influencing the International Migration of Workers." In *Views across the Border: The United States and Mexico*, ed. Stanley R. Ross, pp. 163–180. Albuquerque: University of New Mexico Press.

Marshall, F. Ray, Secretary of Labor; Griffin Bell, Attorney General; and Leonel Castillo, Director of Immigration and Naturalization. 1977. Press Briefing, Office of the White House Press Secretary (August 4).

Mexican American Legal Defense Education Fund. 1977. "Statement of Position Regarding the Administration's Undocumented Alien Legislative Proposal" (November 11).

Midgley, Elizabeth. 1978. "Immigrants: Whose Huddled Masses?" *The Atlantic* 241(4):6–26 (April).

New York Times. 1974a. "Ford Meeting Echeverría at Mexican Border Today" (October 21), p. 1:1.

———. 1974b. "Excerpts from Ford-Echeverría News Conference" (October 22), p. 1:1.

———. 1976. "Ford Signs Immigration Bill Aiding Residents of Western Hemisphere" (October 24), p. 26:4.

———. 1977a. "Zero Population Growth by 2008 is Urged for U.S." (June 24), p. 1-A:14.

———. 1977b. "Aides Say Carter Won't Permit More Mexican Workers in U.S. (July 17).

North, David S. 1971. *Alien Workers: A Study of the Labor Certification Programs*. Washington, D.C.: Trans-Century Corporation.

———. 1977. "Illegal Immigration to the United States: A Quintet of Myths." American Political Science Association, Annual Meeting, Washington, D.C. (September 1–4). [Processed.]

North, David S., and Marion F. Houstoun. 1976. *The Characteristics and Role of Illegal Aliens in the U.S. Labor Market: An Exploratory Study*. Washington, D.C.: Linton & Co.

Piore, Michael J. 1974. "The 'New Immigration' and the Presumptions of Social Policy." *Proceedings of the 27th Annual Winter Meeting*. Industrial Relations Research Association, San Francisco, pp. 350–358.

———. 1975a. "Illegals: Restrictions Aren't the Answer." *New Republic* 172:7–8 (February 22).

———. 1975b. "Impact of Immigration on the Labor Force." *Monthly Labor Review* 98:41–44 (May).

———. 1977. "Undocumented Workers and U.S. Immigration Policy." Panel of the Latin American Studies Association Conference, Houston, Texas (November 4).

Portes, Alejandro. 1974. "Return of the Wetback." *Society* 11(3):40–46 (March–April).

Power, Jonathan. 1978. "Migrant Workers: 'Policy of the Lemon.'" *The Washington Post*, April 8.

Prebisch, Raúl. 1970. *Change and Development: Latin America's Great Task*. Report submitted to the Inter-American Development Bank. Washington, D.C. (July).

Reubens, Edwin P. 1978. "Aliens, Jobs, and Immigration Policy." *The Public Interest* 51:113–134 (Spring).

Riding, Alan. 1977. "Mexican Government's Family Planning Is Making Progress in Lowering Population Growth Rate." *New York Times*, January 9, p. 11:1.

———. 1978. "Silent Invasion: Why Mexico Is an American Problem." *Saturday Review*, July 8, pp. 14–17.

Roberts, Kenneth; Michael Conroy; Allan King; and Jorge Rizo-Patrón. 1978. *The Mexican Migration Numbers Game: An Analysis of the Lesko Estimate of Undocumented Migration from Mexico to the United States*. Austin: Bureau of Business Research, the University of Texas.

Salinas Arizpe, Orel Javier. 1974. *Análisis del efecto de desarrollo económico sobre la distribución del ingreso familiar en México a través de los últimos 25 años; y explicaciones alternativas del comportamiento de dicha distribución durante este período.* Monterrey, Nuevo León: Universidad Autónoma de Nuevo León.

Samora, Julian. 1971. *Los Mojados: The Wetback Story.* Notre Dame, Indiana: University of Notre Dame Press.

———. 1973. "Immigration History Provides Key." *Agenda,* pp. 4–7; 22–23 (Winter).

Shey, Peter. 1977. "Carter's Immigration Proposal: A Windfall for Big Business, Anathema for Undocumented Workers." *Agenda* 7(5):4–15 (September–October).

Smith, B., and R. Newman. 1977. "Depressed Wages along the U.S.-Mexican Border: An Empirical Analysis [bibliography]." *Economic Inquiry* 15:51–66 (January).

Steele, R., and E. Clift. 1977. "Amnesty for Aliens?" *Newsweek* 90:16 (July 4).

Stoddard, Ellwyn R. 1976. "Illegal Mexican Labor in the Borderlands: Institutionalized Support of an Unlawful Practice." *Pacific Sociological Review* 19(2):175–210 (April).

Szulc, Tad. 1978. "Foreign Policy Aspects of the Border." In *Views across the Border: The United States and Mexico,* ed. Stanley R. Ross, pp. 226–238. Albuquerque: University of New Mexico Press.

Ulman, Leon. 1975. "United States Immigration Policies in the Western Hemisphere." Inter-American Bar Association, XIX Conference, Cartagena, Colombia.

U.S. Department of Justice. 1976. *Preliminary Report: Domestic Council Committee on Illegal Aliens.* Washington, D.C.

———. Office of the Attorney General. 1978. "Illegal Immigration: President's Program." Washington, D.C. (April).

U.S. Department of State. Bureau of Public Affairs. 1978. "The Undocumented Aliens Program." GIST document (May).

U.S. News and World Report. 1977a. "Time Bomb in Mexico:

Why There'll Be No End to the Invasion by Illegals; Special Report." 83 : 27–34 (July 4).

———. 1977*b*. "Carter's Plan for Illegal Aliens: Meaning for Business, Workers, Consumers." 83 : 19–20 (August 15).

Urquidi, Victor, and Sofía Méndez Villarreal. 1978. "Economic Importance of Mexico's Northern Border Region." In *Views across the Border: The United States and Mexico*, ed. Stanley R. Ross, pp. 141–162. Albuquerque: University of New Mexico Press.

Villalpando, Vic. et al. 1977. *A Study of the Socioeconomic Impact of Illegal Aliens on the County of San Diego.* San Diego: Human Resources Agency.

Wachter, Michael. 1978. "Second Thoughts about Illegal Immigrants." *Fortune*, May 22, pp. 80–82, 87.

The Wall Street Journal. 1976. "Illegal Alien Non-Problem." Editorial (June 18).

Warren, Robert. 1977. "Recent Immigration and Current Data Collection." *Monthly Labor Review* 100 : 36– 41 (October).

Wierken, Melanie. 1977. "Border Hoppers: Checking the Traffic in Illegal Aliens." *Skeptic* 20 : 44– 47, 59– 60 (July–August).

Wool, Harold. 1976. *The Labor Supply for Lower Level Occupations.* Washington, D.C.: U.S. Department of Labor, R & D Monograph 42.

Zazueta, Carlos H. 1978. "Primera encuesta a trabajadores mexicanos no documentados devueltos de los Estados Unidos octubre–noviembre de 1977: Análisis de algunas variables y cuadros de resultados." Mexico City: Centro Nacional de Información y Estadísticas del Trabajo.